MR. TIM
the Tutor

Inspired by every child
that learns differently

Written By
Kemisha "Mimi"
Swan-Ajayi

Illustrated By
Gaurav Bhatnagar

Mr. Tim The Tutor

First published in 2022

Written by Kemisha Swan-Ajayi

Illustrated and designed by Gaurav Bhatnagar
www.ePublishingexperts.com

ISBN: 979-8-9863155-2-2 (paperback)
       979-8-9863155-3-9 (Hardcover)
       979-8-9863155-4-6 (ebook)

~ **Dedication** ~

This book is dedicated to every child that learns in their own way.

Kemisha L. Swan

Informed by results of a learning disability evaluation. Her school work will become increasingly difficult for her if her basic academic skills are not improved. She will become at risk for dropping out of school if her skills are not improved.

Foster care casenote (1992)

One day, a man named Mr. Tim visited the group home.
I wondered if Mr. Tim knew I lived at the group home with other girls and boys who needed care and support.

I wondered if Mr. Tim knew that the other boys and girls who lived at the group home were like my brothers and sisters, and we were all one BIG happy family.

Did Mr. Tim know my name?
Did Mr. Tim even know how old I was?

My hands began to sweat. I felt really nervous about meeting Mr. Tim for the very first time. I sat quietly in my bedroom waiting for him to arrive.

I looked over at my bed and noticed Mr. Bubbles staring at me. Mr. Bubbles was my BIG brown teddy bear. I got him for my birthday last year.

Mr. Tim pulled out the chair next to me and sat down.
I noticed he was carrying a black briefcase.
"Again, I'm Mr. Tim. Now, what is your name?"

"My name is Mimi. I am eight years old, and that's Mr. Bubbles," I said as I sat up and pointed.

"Well, it's nice to meet you and your friend," Mr. Tim said as he shook my hand and waved at Mr. Bubbles. "I'm your new tutor," Mr. Tim said.
"Tutor! What's a tutor?" I asked quickly.

"Well, a tutor is sort of like a teacher. Someone who helps you learn and understand something new," Mr. Tim explained.
Will Mr. Tim teach me how to read better? Will he teach me how to spell my name? I wondered.

"Okay, shall we start?" Mr. Tim asked. He reached inside his black briefcase and pulled out a notebook and a pen. "Let me start by asking you this. Do you know which is your right hand and which is your left?" Mr. Tim asked.

"No. I MEAN, YES!" I said, hoping Mr. Tim would ask me another question. I was too ashamed to tell him that I really didn't know my right hand from my left hand.

"Okay, good! Can you raise your right hand for me?" Mr. Tim asked.
I slowly raised one hand. I didn't know whether the hand I raised was my right hand or left hand.

Mr. Tim wrote in his notebook.
"That's your left hand. BUT don't feel bad, Mimi. This is why I'm here to help you."
Mr. Tim could tell I felt really sad.

"Well, it's not my fault I need more help than the other kids in my class!" I said as I put my head back on the desk. "I can't learn like they do."

Mr. Tim patted me on the shoulder. "Cheer up," he said.
"Some people just learn in different ways, and that's okay! Do you want me to make those silly faces again?"

Mr. Tim stuck his tongue out and twisted both of his thumbs against his cheeks. No matter how hard I tried, I couldn't stop myself from laughing. I looked at Mr. Tim with the biggest smile on my face.

"I am going to teach you a trick. It's going to help you learn your right hand from your left hand," Mr. Tim said as he placed his pen inside his notebook.

"Do you mean the kind of trick where a bunny comes out of a hat?" I asked.
Mr. Tim laughed, "No, silly."

"Raise the hand you write with," Mr. Tim said.
I did what Mr. Tim asked me to do.
"What if I told you the hand you raised is ALWAYS going to be your RIGHT hand," Mr. Tim said. "And If you forget, just remember your RIGHT hand is the same as your WRITE hand."

"Wow! Well, that was easy," I said. I looked at Mr. Bubbles, and back at Mr. Tim. I couldn't believe Mr. Tim taught me a new trick, and now I was ready to teach Mr. Bubbles.

"Now, Mimi, raise your right hand," Mr. Tim said. With a HUGE smile on my face, I proudly raised my right hand.

Mr. Tim never treated me differently, even though it took me longer to learn new things.

Mr. Tim made learning fun, and taught Mr. Bubbles and I many other tricks to help me learn in my own way. Mr. Tim was my favorite tutor.

Every child is one caring adult away from being a success story

~ Josh Shipp ~

About the Author

Kemisha "Mimi" Swan-Ajayi grew up in Chicago's foster care community in a group home. It was then that she was diagnosed with a learning disability and was assigned a gentle, kind and patient tutor, Mr. Tim. He became a pivotal figure in her life and instilled confidence in her abilities.

She credits her teachers, social workers, and foster parents who taught her the value and impact of education, and helped her become the first in her family to graduate college and discover her passion for writing.

Kemisha lives in Evanston with her husband and two children. She currently attends graduate school to become a school social worker, and also works as an Education Support Professional with special education students in her hometown school district.

"I'm dedicating this book to my family and to every child who learns differently, and to every educator who teaches students in many diverse learning styles. My students and my children inspired me to write it."

She thanks her husband and children for their love and support, and her co-workers in education for believing in her vision.

Made in the USA
Monee, IL
03 February 2023

27064650R00017